Tim Burton's Corpse Bride

Alfred Publishing Co., Inc.
16320 Roscoe Blvd., Suite 100
P.O. Box 10003
Van Nuys, CA 91410-0003
alfred.com

ISBN-10: 0-7390-4695-0
ISBN-13: 978-0-7390-4695-1

MW00795617

Contents

VICTOR'S PIANO SOLO

Music by DANNY ELFMAN

(cluster chords)

*F♯✕ = G♮

CORPSE BRIDE (MAIN TITLE)

Music by DANNY ELFMAN

REMAINS OF THE DAY

Additional Lyrics by
JOHN AUGUST

Music and Lyrics by
DANNY ELFMAN

Moderately bright ♩ = 160

Bone Jangles:

1. Hey,—

Verse 1:

give me a lis - ten, you corp - ses of cheer,— at least those of you who

still got an ear.— I'll tell you a sto - ry, make a skel - e - ton cry,— of our

Bm Cdim7 C#7

just could-n't cope,___ so our lov-ers came up with a plan to e - lope.

Chorus:
Am
Everybody:
E7 Am

Die, die, we all pass a - way,___ but don't wear a frown___ 'cause it's

E7 F6 E7 F E7

real - ly o - kay.___ You might try and hide,___ and you might try and pray,___ but we

Am Am(maj7)/G# Am7/G F E7

all end up the re - mains of the day.___ Yeah, yeah, yeah, yeah,___ yeah.

Moderately ♩ = 92 (♫ = ♪³♪)

Bridge:

con-jured up a plan to meet late at night. They told not a soul, kept the whole thing tight. Now her

moth-er's wed-ding dress fit like a glove. You don't need much when you're real-ly in love, ex -

cept for a few things, or so I'm told, like the fam - i - ly jewels and a satch-el of gold. Then

next to the grave-yard by the old oak tree, on a dark fog-gy night at a quar-ter to three, she was

ACCORDING TO PLAN

Lyrics by JOHN AUGUST
and DANNY ELFMAN

Music by DANNY ELFMAN

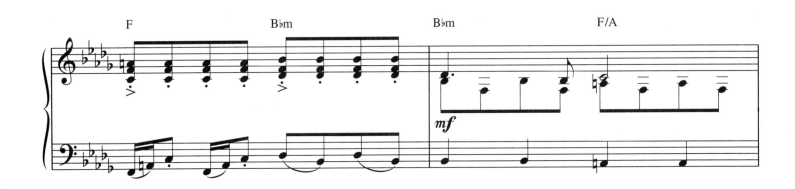

According to Plan - 10 - 1
27925

Moderately slow ♩ = 80

28

According to Plan - 10 - 9
27925

TEARS TO SHED

Additional Lyrics by
JOHN AUGUST

Music and Lyrics by
DANNY ELFMAN

Moderately slow ♩ = 72

Verse 1:

1. What does that wisp-y lit-tle brat have that you don't have dou-ble? She

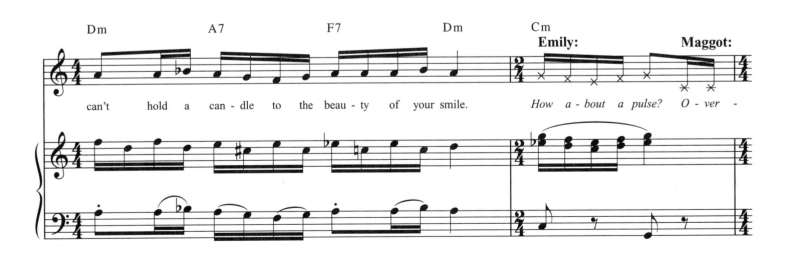

can't hold a can-dle to the beau-ty of your smile. *How a-bout a pulse? O-ver-*

32

A little faster ♩ = 80

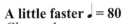
Chorus 1:

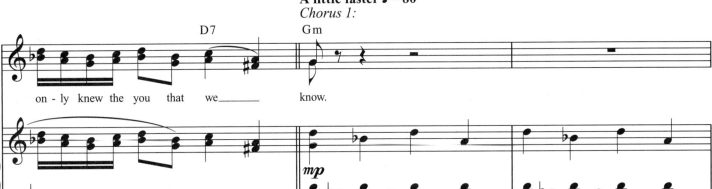

only knew the you that we_____ know.

Emily:

1. If I touch a burn-ing can-dle, I can feel no pain. If you

cut me with a knife, it's still the same. And I

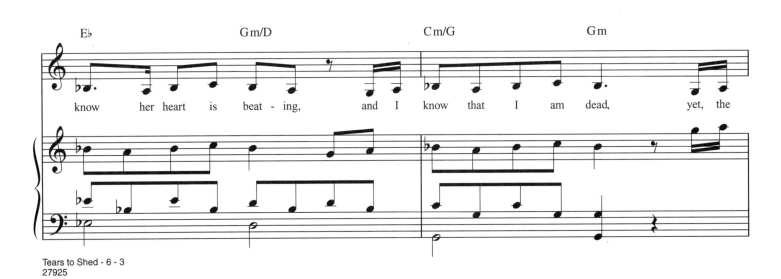

know her heart is beat-ing, and I know that I am dead, yet, the

Tears to Shed - 6 - 3
27925

THE PIANO DUET

Secondo

Music by DANNY ELFMAN

Slowly, freely (♩. = 44)

The Piano Duet - 6 - 1
27925

THE PIANO DUET

Primo

Music by DANNY ELFMAN

Slowly, freely (♩. = 44)

The Piano Duet - 6 - 2
27925

38

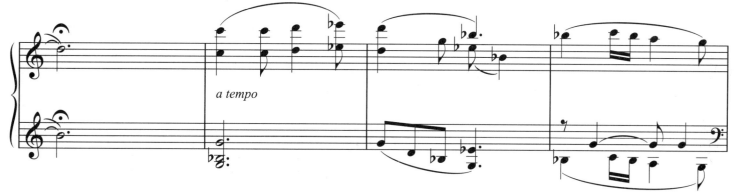

The Piano Duet - 6 - 4
27925

40

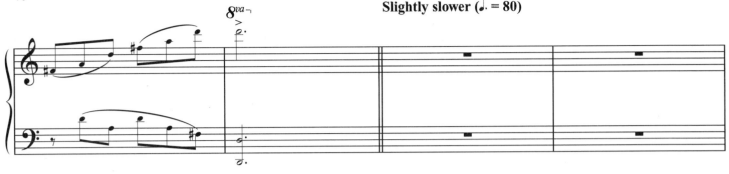

Slightly slower (♩. = 80)

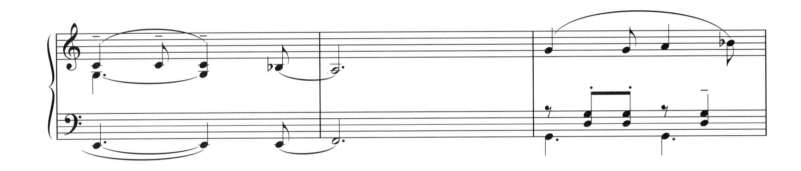

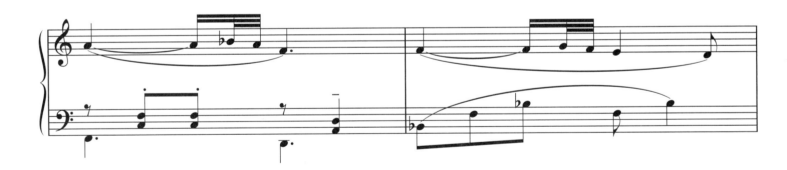

The Piano Duet - 6 - 5
27925

Slightly slower (♩. = 80)

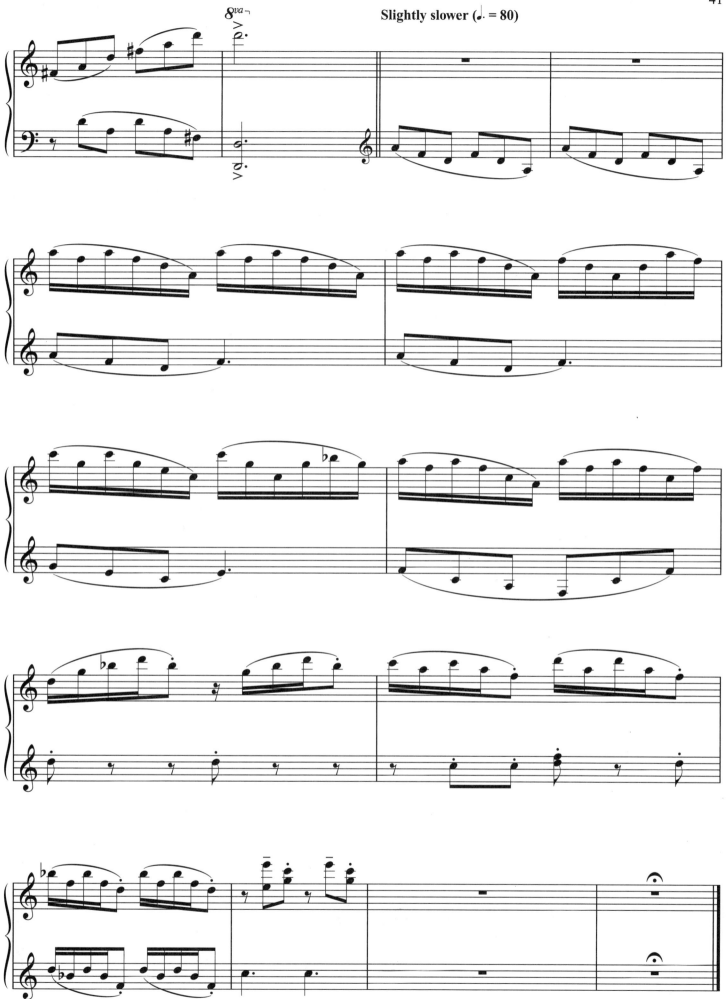

THE WEDDING SONG

Music and Lyrics by
DANNY ELFMAN

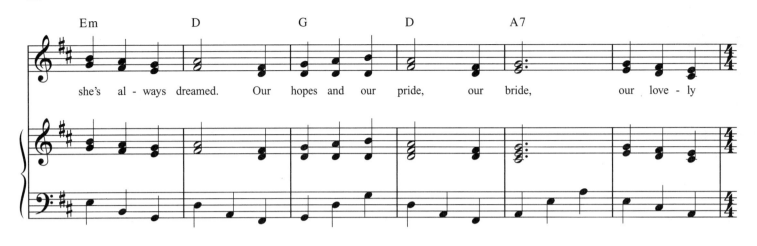

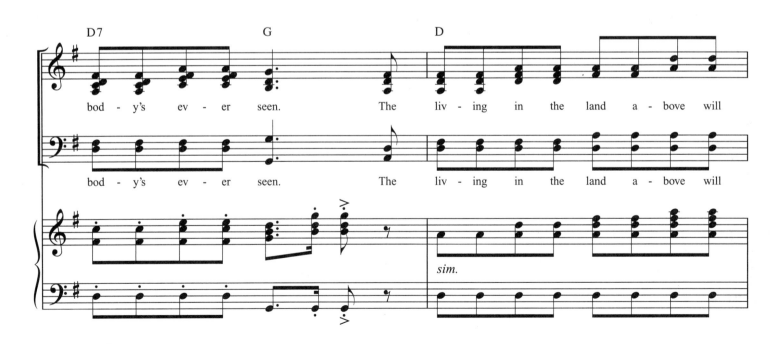

2

BALL & SOCKET LOUNGE MUSIC #1
(Band Version)

Music by DANNY ELFMAN

Moderate swing ♩ = 126

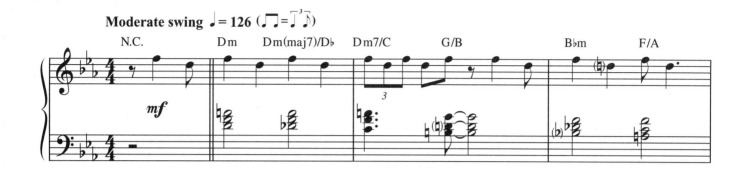

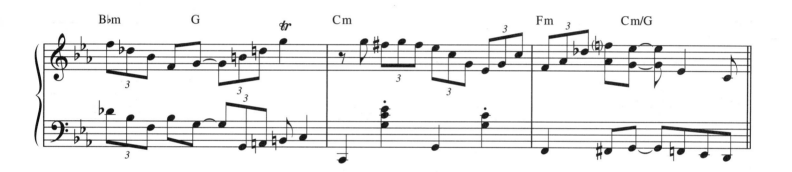

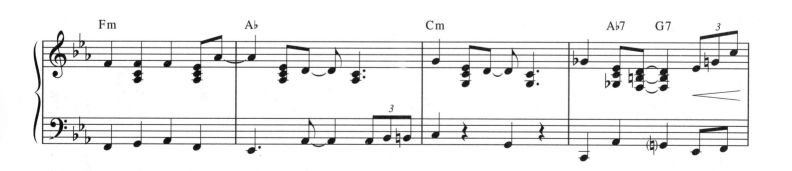

BALL & SOCKET LOUNGE MUSIC #2

Music by DANNY ELFMAN

Ball & Socket Lounge Music #2 - 3 - 2
27925

REMAINS OF THE DAY
(Combo Lounge version - Piano solo excerpt)

Music by DANNY ELFMAN

Moderately fast shuffle ♩ = 132

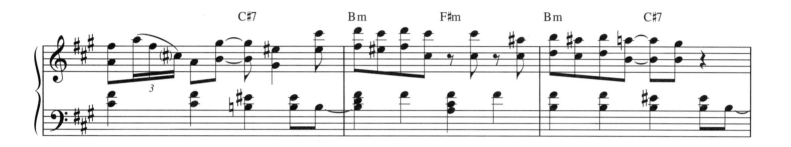

Remains of the Day - 2 - 1
27925

62

(end solo)

Remains of the Day - 2 - 2
27925